Old PORTRUSH, BUSHMILLS and the GIA̶N̶T̶'S̶ CAUSEWAY

by
Alex F. Young

The railway station and town hall at Portrush, 1927.

First published in the United Kingdom, 2002,
by Stenlake Publishing,
Telephone / Fax: 01290 551122

ISBN 1 84033 189 5

FURTHER READING

The books listed below were used by the author during his research. None of them are available from Stenlake Publishing. Those interested in finding out more are advised to contact their local bookshop or reference library.
Bushmills: Conservation Village, Department of the Environment, 1992.
Spirit of the Age: The Story of Old Bushmills, Alf McCreary, Old Bushmills Distillery Company Ltd, 1983.
The Giant's Causeway Tramway, J.H. McGuigan, Oakwood Press, 1963.
The Giant's Causeway, The National Trust (Education).
Portrush Heroes, 1914–1918, Robert Thompson, 2001.

ACKNOWLEDGEMENTS

The author wishes to thank Peter Bolan, Lil McKillop, David Speirs of Causeway Books, Alan Dunlop of the Bushmills Inn, Dr Liam O'Connor, Ian Stewart, Arnaldo Morelli, Alex Duncan of Seabank Residential Home, Acky Colgan, Rev. Bert Montgomery, Mrs R. Armstrong of the Causeway Hotel, John Scott, Robert Sharpe, Robert Thompson, Eamonn Brolly, Albert Rohdich, Nicola McCullough of the National Trust, Hugh McGrattan of the *Coleraine Chronicle*, Tony Ellis of HM Coastguard, Brenda Collins of the Irish Linen Centre and Lisburn Museum, Glenda Rodgers, Rita Harkin of the Ulster Architectural Heritage Society, and Jim Allen of the Causeway Coast Maritime Heritage Group.

The publishers wish to thank Eddie Mason for permission to reproduce the photographs on pages 5, 6, 9 and 18.

Weaving's days as a cottage industry had long gone by the time of this photograph from the early 1900s, but not the specialist craft of embroidery, as this advertising picture used by the Irish Embroidery Depot at 3 Main Street, Portrush, illustrates. Known as 'whitework', items were commissioned from local women by agents of drapers' firms and warehouses, usually in Derry or Belfast. The women worked at home and earnings were extremely low. Common between 1870 and 1930, the main centres of 'whitework' were Co. Donegal and Co. Derry. Portrush was not a major producer although from the point of view of delivery and despatch, the railway was obviously of great benefit.

INTRODUCTION

PORTRUSH

From early times Portrush was a harbour, or more correctly, a landing place, around which grew a scattering of fishermen's cottages. By the late eighteenth century it had one merchant and an inn. Trade and development came with the decision in 1826 by the Portrush Harbour Company to build a true harbour. Thereafter, growing tourist interest in the Giant's Causeway brought steamer services with Liverpool and Glasgow and assured the town's future. The arrival of the railway in 1855 brought more tourists and the need to accommodate them resulted in more building. The benefits of the tramway to Bushmills in 1883, and to the Giant's Causeway four years later, were not immediate, but in 1899 it carried 95,151 passengers. As the nineteenth century closed Portrush had at least seventeen hotels and many, many boarding houses. Tourism had now supplanted both harbour trade and fishing.

Cassell's *Gazetteer of Great Britain and Ireland*, published in 1900, described Portrush as a 'seaport and fashionable watering place'. However, during the First World War the boat service to Scotland was stopped and income from tourism was halved. It would never really recover. Efforts were made in the 1920s and '30s – Barry's Amusements (including the 1935 indoor entertainment area), the Arcadia Dance Hall and Phil's Amusements were all successful ventures – but the high season was gone. The closure of the tramway in 1949 seemed the final nail in the coffin and the 1950s, '60s and the 'troubles' of the '70s merely confirmed this. Portrush was not unique during these times, as the history of any British resort during the rise of the Spanish resorts will show. Only since the late 1980s has tourism – on the back of golf weeks (the Senior British Open Championship in 1995, '96 and '97), motor cycle racing, soccer tournaments and sea angling – started its recovery and found its future.

THE TRAMWAY

The Giant's Causeway, Portrush and Bush Valley Railway and Tramway Co. Ltd came into being through the efforts of Dr Anthony Traill, a Fellow of Trinity College, Dublin, and his brother William Atcheson Traill, at a public meeting in Bushmills in October 1879. As a geologist, William Traill knew of the area's rich mineral deposits – iron ore, gravel, basalt, limestone and sand – which could be exploited in tandem with passenger transport. In September 1880, with parliamentary approval and capital of £20,000 in their pocket, the Traills saw the first sod cut of their 3 foot gauge line from Portrush to Bushmills. This line would be different from most others, harnessing electrical power from a generating station on the river at Bushmills. However, these were experimental times (the only other electric tram in Britain was the half mile stretch along Brighton Esplanade) and when the line opened on 29 January 1883 steam traction was used. The inaugural electric powered run came eight months later, on 28 September, with regular services starting in the November. The system's initial rolling stock consisted of two steam locomotives, seven passenger trailers, and twelve goods wagons – but no electric cars. Four were delivered the following year. It was inevitable that the burgeoning tourist business would push the line to the Giant's Causeway and on 1 July 1887 the extended line was opened. The hoped for revenue from mineral transportation failed to materialise, but the summer passenger traffic almost compensated for this. Over the years, as the system and trams aged, maintenance costs mounted, and it was only due to the arrival of American servicemen during the Second World War and the introduction of winter schedules that the company survived until 1949.

BUSHMILLS

With the River Bush dividing it between the parishes of Billy on the east and Dunluce to the west, Bushmills was known in the seventeenth century as Portcamon, but if one thinks of the town's name as 'the mills on the Bush' the change is understandable. The Ordnance Survey map of 1902 shows the river powering two flax mills, two corn mills, a saw mill, a paper mill and a spade mill. Sir Francis Workman Macnaghten of Bushmills House started the town's development in the 1820s with a market held on Tuesdays and Fridays, a corn store, a courthouse and a hotel. Across the new bridge, which brought the Dunluce road into Main Street in the 1840s, came the development of Market Square. Its pseudo Round Tower was built in 1874 and the cenotaph was erected in the 1920s. One by one the mills fell into disuse, but in the days before visitor centres and the whiskey distillery, which has done rather well in promoting Bushmills' name around the world, the village survived thanks to the Giant's Causeway. Bushmills now falls within a designated Area of Outstanding Beauty and is protected as a World Heritage Site with almost ninety listed buildings.

THE GIANT'S CAUSEWAY

Sixty million years ago the north Antrim coast went through periods of extensive, if not spectacular, volcanic activity, building up five or six layers of basalt. Some of this lava cooled into a crystalline form and some into polygonal columns. The Causeway's 'discovery' in 1693, and its first appearance on a map twenty years later, created intense interest and debate as to how it was formed. Was it natural or man-made? Of course, we now know that Finn McCool played no part in what was a wholly natural phenomenon. By the mid-nineteenth century it had an economy of its own, with guides, boatmen, stall holders and photographers; and, from the 1890s until the 1960s, an entry charge was made. Only when it was taken over by the National Trust in 1961 was all of this cleared away and an appropriate visitors' centre built. In 1986 it was one of thirty-one sites added to the UNESCO (United Nations Educational, Scientific and Cultural Organization) World Heritage List, affording it special protection.

Station Square and Eglinton Street, Portrush, viewed from Kerr Street late on a summer's evening in the early years of the twentieth century. Much has changed. The terrace of fine houses which extends from the left behind the drinking fountain are now shops, although the Eglinton Hotel, past Dunluce Avenue, is still there.

Dating from 1933, this view of Portrush takes in the railway station, the Golf Hotel (or was it still then the Hydropathic Hotel?) and the developing housing estate of Dhu Varren ('the dark rocks') across the bay. The railway line from Belfast to Ballymena opened in 1848, but took another seven years to reach Portrush via Ballymoney and Coleraine. In 1860 the line was taken over by the Belfast and Northern Counties Railway. The original station, which had only one platform, was rebuilt in 1893 in grand Tudor Style. It had three 600 foot long platforms, the first third of which were covered, a 6,000 square foot booking hall, and an adjoining café/restaurant which could cater for 300. The station cost £10,000. To encourage development in Portrush, anyone building a house with an annual value in excess of £25 was offered free first class travel to Belfast for ten years. These 'Villa Tickets' helped treble the town's population to 1,800 in the fifty years up to 1895, and summer visitors quadrupled this figure. While the main building still stands, the station is now a shadow of its former self. On her granite plinth, in the centre of the picture, stands Victory, Portrush's war memorial. Commissioned by a special committee formed in 1920, it commemorates the seventy-eight Portrush men who fell in the First World War and was sculpted by Frank Ransom of Golders Green in London. It was unveiled on Armistice Day 1922. Thirty more names were added after the end of the Second World War.

With the exception of the Golf Hotel, now Castle Erin, this view is of times past. On the left is the veranda of the Station Dining Rooms, the Railway Station with carriages in the siding, and the American Skating Rink. Arriving from America at the turn of the century, roller skating rinks epitomised a new age and proliferated throughout the country. Portrush's opened in 1905. The £5,000 rink was vast, measuring 200 by 60 foot and illuminated by a generator from Curran Bros. of Belfast. Few of the skaters at this time would have electricity in their homes. This rink was one of many built by Messrs T. Anderson of Lagan Works, Belfast, to a design by J.S. Kennedy of Coleraine. As the rink could accommodate 2,000 skaters, its proximity to the railway station was no accident. From this short-lived craze local man Stanley Harper is remembered as 'artistry on skates'. After serving as an army billet during the First World War, financial difficulties caused its closure shortly afterwards. It was then demolished. The timber was taken around the bay and rose again in the new wooden housing development at Dhu Varren. The site of the rink is now home to Barry's Super-Loop roller coaster.

Idle taxis in Station Square, 1927. Private cars were not permitted in the square. Although part of the railway station, the café was used by townspeople during winter months as a meeting place and badminton court. Requisitioned during the Second World War, it was both a lecture hall and a billet for American forces. It is said that the Americans discovered the liquor store in the basement, and also became masters with the hook and line. Beyond, where the fairground would later stand, is wind-blown sand and the harbour with its loading hopper (which is in the centre of the picture). The hopper was built in 1911 and used a system of buckets and shutes to load locally quarried road metal onto ships which had arrived with Scottish coal. It was demolished in the early 1970s. Today, it would have been saved by the industrial archaeological interest its unique design would have attracted.

From Station Square, this view takes in the Town Hall, to the right, and the length of Kerr Street (Harbour Road) towards the harbour and Ramore Head. The overhead power pole followed the sweep of the tramway from the railway station into Eglinton Street enroute to the Causeway. Described as 'an immensely vigorous high-Victorian building', the red brick Town Hall was built in 1872 to a design by the architects Lanyon, Lynn and Lanyon. (With offices in Belfast and Dublin, this partnership was formed in 1860 when Charles Lanyon and William Henry Lynn took in Lanyon's eldest son John, but was dissolved in July 1872 following a court action by Lynn.) In 1999 the building's future became uncertain with Coleraine Borough Council deciding that as a high proportion of its brickwork was irreparable it should be demolished. The Ulster Architectural Heritage Society successfully contested this decision and the building was saved.

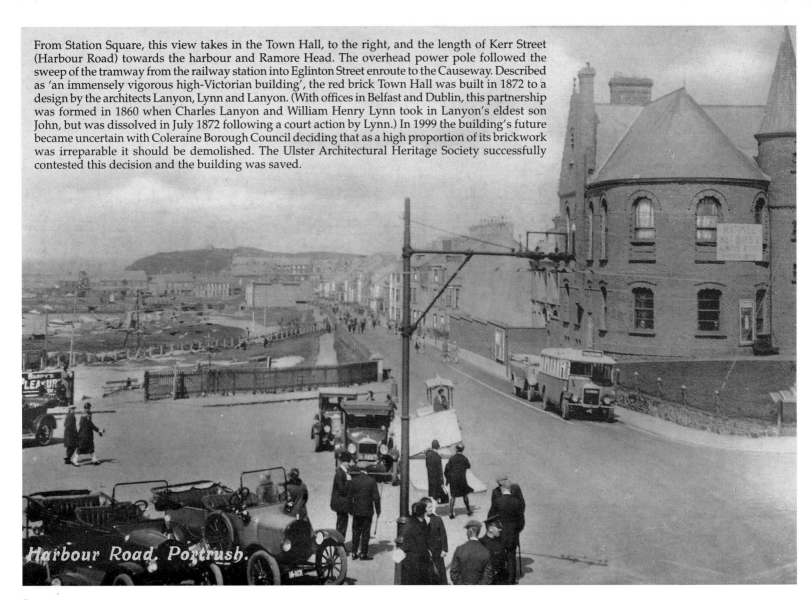

Harbour Road, Portrush.

Kerr Street, seen here in Edwardian times, grew from discrete developments started about 1840. The properties behind are in Mark Street. With the town established as a popular holiday resort, there emerged class divisions amongst the visiting clientele and those providing accommodation. For example, most houses would have catered for 'holidaymakers', while the Victoria Hotel on the left (now Rogues Wine Bar) would have thought of itself as attracting 'guests'. Tramlines can just be seen, with an end of line buffer just above the quayside fuel tank. The low building beyond the south quay wall belonged to the tramway.

This view looks south from Main Street towards Eglinton Street (with the railway station clock tower) which brought the tramway from the railway station to turn right into Causeway Street. On the junction stands the Dr Adam Clarke Memorial Methodist Church, designed by Thomas Eliot of Enniskillen and opened on 29 September 1887 to replace the 1832 church building. Dr Adam Clarke (*c.*1762–1832), to whom the church is dedicated, was a native of Portstewart who converted to Methodism in 1778. He is remembered for his eight volume *Commentary on the Bible* (published between 1810 and 1826). He presented the church with its bell which had been cast by Francis Fremy at Amsterdam in 1681. After passing through the hands of the tsar of Russia, it was gifted to Clarke who in turn presented it to the church. Sadly, with its housing in the belfry no longer secure, it was brought down some years ago. The obelisk erected to Clark's memory in 1859 stood on a banking behind the church until 1910 when it was resited at the front. One of the Urban Council's conditions for allowing electrification of the line through the town was that the pole 'at the Methodist Church bend was illuminated' during the hours of darkness.

A tram trundles down Causeway Street, making for Bushmills and the Causeway. Today the street lights are electric powered sodium/mercury tubes and the overhead tram power lines have gone – and, of course, fashions are a little different. However, the street looks very much the same. The postcard from which this illustration comes was printed in Berlin, and posted in Portrush on 8 July 1917 to a Miss Hammond in Davenport. The sender, 'LAK', wrote 'Down here for the weekend. I didn't know this was a German card until I had it bought. So don't tell anyone.'

Main Street, with the Atlantic Avenue and the Londonderry Hotel which was famed for its Trocadero tea dances. In later years the White House department store, which was to survive the Londonderry, had a 'Trocadero' restaurant.

Photographed from Castle Erin, this panoramic view shows the busy railway station and Eglinton Street, which by the early twentieth century would have been taken up with boarding houses. Beyond the houses, the East Strand stretches out to Dunluce Castle and Benbane Head.

LADIES BATHING PLACE, PORTRUSH.

01293

The Ladies' Bathing Place. The pathway in the upper left of the picture winds down from Bath Terrace and the Seabank Hotel, passing the salmon fishery buildings and into the ladies' bathing cove, with the Skerries off shore. On the right, where the Arcadia would later stand, are the ramshackle ladies' changing facilities and kiosks.

The 1920s brought the jewel in Portrush's crown of attractions – the Arcadia Café, which was built by local businessman, R.A. Chalmers. The Ulster Architectural Heritage Society describes it as, 'a mannerist stucco palais, worthy of the promenade at Nice and firmly founded upon a rock'. Over the years, the rock has been the one piece of stability it has had, but it still evokes memories of summer evening dances on the upper, open-air floor, and, for children of the time, the rich aroma of candy floss.

By the time of this 1936 photograph the Arcadia had developed into the form which is recognisable today. Between then and now, however, a large new ballroom has come and gone at the right hand side. The building is currently undergoing restoration to become a café again.

Another view from 1934, taken from the end of Bath Terrace, shows best why the Arcadia stood out, and why, for a period, it was so successful. In the late 1940s and early 50s, David Glover and his orchestra added to its popularity. In the summer seasons of those years, Joe Loss and his band were also regulars as well as the Scottish entertainers, Andy Stewart and Robert Wilson.

The band strikes up in Antrim Gardens Park in the days before the First World War. Beyond, Causeway View comes in from the left, turning into Lansdowne Road.

Surprisingly little is known of the Portrush Hydropathic and Golf Hotel which stands between the railway station, to which there was a footbridge, and the sea, other than its ties with golf and the spa. The course traded on the promise that you could tee off within ten minutes of stepping from the train. It is now the Castle Erin Christian Holiday and Conference Centre.

On Main Street, at its corner with Mark Street, today's Comfort Hotel has a history reaching back to 1837 when a Dr Boyd opened Portrush's first hotel, the Antrim Arms, which then consisted of the three storey, double bayed, right hand end. In 1892 it was bought by the Belfast and Northern Counties Railway and reconstructed and extended to a plan by the architect Lanyon. His use of the French style is unmistakable. In today's Belfast, everyone's grandfather supposedly worked on the *Titanic*, but the 'Northern Counties' ballroom was actually hung with curtains intended for the ship. With its oak-lined reception area, grand stairways and chandeliers, it was the height of grand Victorian taste. After a fire in 1991, the shell of the building was used for the new Comfort Hotel.

Now the Seabank Residential Home, this photograph shows this Italianate Bath Terrace villa in the early twentieth century when it was the fifty-bed Seabank Hotel (run from 1915 by Miss Emily Fitzpatrick). It was built as a boarding house in 1890 by John Hetherington, on a plot of ground extending back to Main Street which he took on a ninety-nine year lease from Lord Antrim. The legend that the earl built the house as a summer retreat is without foundation. After serving the Methodist Church as a hall of residence, it fell into dereliction until 1989 when redevelopment transformed it into the residential home.

This photograph, and the two which follow, show Portrush Harbour around 1905. This was its heyday when passenger ships vied with merchantmen and fishermen, and sail vied with steam. In this summer view another crowd of passengers would have been about to spill onto the quay from the SS *Shamrock* which would have left Ardrossan in Scotland early that morning. Built at Glasgow in 1879, the 231 foot long Shamrock was one of five Laird Line ships operating on this route. She was wrecked off Lanby Island, Dublin, in 1918. The bridge across the inner basin, built in the 1860s, carried the railway line to the harbour. It proved too light for the later, heavier, locomotives, and wagons were then winched across. The present bridge was built in 1980.

The harbour viewed from the south, taking in the row of buildings on the north quay and Ramore Head beyond. The fishing smacks are typical, as is the two masted schooner berthed at the quay. With a capacity of between 50 and 70 tons, this would have plied between Portrush and the Clyde ports in Scotland, taking freestone and basalt from the Giant's Causeway, and returning with coal. Built in the 1830s, the grain store to the right of the smacks was for many years used by the grain merchants Spiller and Baker of Liverpool. It is now used by Portrush Yacht Club.

The Laird Line ship, SS *Olive* (sister ship to the *Shamrock*), departing for Ardrossan. Built in 1893, she was withdrawn from service in 1930. The coach and wagon, pictured above the coal on the dockside, shows the railway was still in service. This view also shows the lines of the harbour as laid out by the distinguished port engineer, Sir John Rennie. A Scot who was knighted in recognition of his work on London Bridge, he was commissioned by the Portrush Harbour Company in 1826 to build the eight acre site. Costing £1,600, the finance was raised in £100 shares mainly from Coleraine merchants. The one time draught of 27 feet is now only 7 feet.

As the Urban Council struggled to increase Portrush's popularity as a seaside resort with bigger and better attractions, one simple attraction came when seabathing moved from the realm of therapy to the world of recreation. Today, the 1920s stairways, boardwalks and huts look primitive – as does the idea of bathing in the cold waters of the North Atlantic!

The popularity of the Pool for boating is shown by this photograph which appeared on a postcard the boat hire company cleverly used as a ticket to show the times of the hire.

This early photograph shows Tram no. 4 and its trailer at the passing loop on the tramway which overlooked Dunluce Castle. Parallel to the track ran the power rail, the forerunner of the overhead lines. Surrounded on three sides by 100 foot cliffs, the castle entered recorded history when it was attacked by the Norwegian Magnus Barefoot in the twelfth century. Cooney O'Flynn then held the castle. How it would have looked at that time is unknown, but building and expansion would have continued through the centuries as it passed from owner to owner. The last occupants, the McQuillans, lost it after suffering defeat at the hands of the McDonnell family and this led to its complete abandonment. It remains one of the most picturesque ruins in Ireland.

Ready to pull away from the Causeway Terminus with Bob Scott at the controls, Tram no. 23, with two covered toast racks in tow, was about to head back to Portrush. Acquired in 1908, its wooden, awning style roof was supported on iron stanchions. Bob worked with the tramway most of his days, becoming its general factotum. Every working day he started at eight o'clock, checking each tram for oil and grease. Acting as a driver during the busy summer period, he also maintained the system in winter. Both he and his son Archie worked with the trams until 1949. Bob died at his home in Bushmills in December 1952, having survived the tramway's demise by three years.

Tram no. 22, pictured in July 1933 with Dan Jamieson at the controls and William Glass as conductor. Brought into service in 1902, this seven bench toast rack was similar to numbers 20 and 21, and brought the rolling stock to three electric cars and eighteen trailers. Dan died at his home in Ballyness in the 1960s; William set up a bicycle business in what is now the Bushmills Inn.

Delivered between 1888 and 1890 as an enclosed trailer, no. 9 was converted to power in 1909 and had the added luxury of a glazed cab for the driver. Uniquely, it was divided into First and Ordinary sections. With two toastracks in tow, it pulls off along Eglinton Street on a summer's afternoon – a day for the open carriages. Has the driver spotted someone in the street or run over someone on the track? Opposite, on the Dunluce Street corner, stands Morelli's Savoy Café. From the province of Frosinone in Italy's Abruzza mountains, the Morelli family came to Britain with their recipe for ice cream and settled in Greenock, Scotland. Four of their seven sons came to Northern Ireland and opened cafés in Coleraine, Ballymena and Strabane, as well as the Savoy in Portrush.

Trams nos. 20 and 21, purchased for the opening of the overhead system in July 1899, stand outside the depot at Portrush, which was built of basalt rubble and could accommodate eighteen cars. When new these two seven bench toastracks brought the rolling stock up to three steam locomotives, four electric cars and seventeen trailers. Driver Robert Sharpe, who worked on the trams from 1942 until the end in 1949, stands in the cab of no. 21. Both of these trams would end their days on Johnny Armour's farm at Bushmills.

As the 10.15 a.m. tram, no. 21, pulls up the hill out of Portrush the canvas screens suggest that the weather prospects on Wednesday, 5 May 1920 (when this photograph was taken) were not good.

This early twentieth century photograph of the Old Bushmills Distillery shows one stage in the programme of development and building which began after the fire of 25 November 1885. 'The spirit obtained by distillation from a mash of cereal grains saccharified by the diastase of malt', better known as whiskey (the misspelled one comes from the other side of the North Channel), has a history in Ireland dating back to the sixth century. By comparison, Bushmills Distillery is fairly new, initially only gaining a seven year distilling licence from King James I on 20 April, 1608. The premises lost in the fire were of wooden buildings and thatched roofs and a typical nineteenth century disaster waiting to happen. In the rebuild, local stone and, later, brick were used. One distinctive feature missing from this scene are the two pagoda roofed kilns which were completed by 1922.

Bushmills in the days when the River Bush had to work its passage through the village. This view, down to the bridge which carries Bridge Street onto Main Street, shows on the left the outflow of the lade from the corn mill. Of the two wheels across the river, again served by a lade, the one to the left was Palmers Corn Mill, which dates from the 1860s, while the one to the right served a sawmill. Whether or not the angler made a catch he would have been glad to learn that where the photographer stood is now the River Bush Salmon Station. Under the management of the Department of Agriculture for Northern Ireland, the station's hatchery can hold eight million green ova and two million hatching ova, while its forty-two tank rearing area has the capacity for 22,000 salmon smolts and 3,000 broodstock adults.

Bridge Street, or Church Street as it was known at the time of this photograph, sweeps down past the Cottage Hospital on the left and across the bridge to Main Street. Dates for the hospital could not be found, although it appears as such on the 1902 map. It is remembered from the 1940s as William and Cathie Boyle's house. William, the Church of Ireland caretaker, rented the left front room to St John's Church each week for their Sunday school. The house was demolished in the early 1950s and replaced by a modern terrace. The building across the river once housed the bank, but is currently planned to become 'a prime riverfront development opportunity in a courtyard style setting'. Of the buildings in Main Street, the shop on the left is now an office (McAlister and Anderson, accountants) and the pub on the right became the Distillers Arms in 1995. A one-time farmhouse, this has also been the premises of Nichol's Bar and the Bridgend Bar.

Bushmills' Main Street in the late nineteenth century. The wall on the left enclosed pastureland where the telephone exchange is now, while the Masonic Hall (Lodge 414, Royal Blue), the Methodist church and the terraced houses run towards Market Square and its distinctive replica Irish round tower. On the right stands Kane's Commercial and Family Hotel (it is said to have had a pub with very flexible hours). The building dates from the 1820s and is now the Bushmills Inn. On the footpath by the door causeway stones can be seen.

MAIN STREET, BUSHMILLS.

This mid-1890s photograph, one of the earliest of the Main Street, shows Bushmills on a monthly fair day. While the weekly markets (Tuesday and Friday) were for fruit, vegetables and hardware such as pots and pans, the fair was for horses, carts and, at times, even servants (who at that time were often engaged for work at hiring fairs). There being no coal gas, carbide was used in the street lighting.

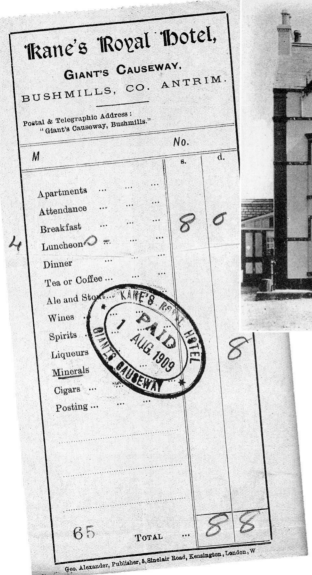

The Kane family are said to have owned this hotel, the Royal (built in 1863), and the Causeway Hotel. There may also have been a connection with Kane's Family and Commercial Hotel in Bushmills. As Prince of Wales, King Edward VII (1841–1910) is credited with putting the 'Royal' into Kane's Hotel, having been invited to afternoon tea during a visit to the Causeway. It was owned by Colin Kane when demolished in the early 1960s.

We can presume that this receipt from Kane's Royal Hotel was not presented to a royal visitor and his party.

Established as an inn by a Miss Henry during the 1830s, the Causeway Hotel retained its 'elite' custom, even when Kane's became 'Royal'. One nineteenth century owner, William McNaul, traded on the promise to 'do all in his power to promote the comfort of his guests'. Built in 1836 as an inn, possibly called the 'Red House', business from Causeway visitors grew at such a pace that it developed into a thirty-two bedroom hotel (it now has twenty-eight bedrooms). When William Traill, having built the Causeway tramway, bought the hotel, it became the first in Ireland to have electric power. This was tapped from the tramway system at a charge of £10 per annum. The Pagoda Tea Room, to the right of the hotel, was a favourite summer evening rendezvous.

The waters off the north Antrim coast have always been a rich fishing ground with boats from Portstewart, Portrush and Dunseverick harvesting lobster and crab from the shoreline, and cod and plaice from deeper water beyond. But since the seventeenth century, something unique has been exploited at Carraig-a-Rade (or Carrick-a-Rede) – 'the rock of the open anchorage'. Atlantic salmon returning to spawn in the River Bush and the River Bann are carried easterly towards the Kintyre peninsula where they turn south into the North Channel, through Rathlin Sound, and past Carrick-a-Rede. Accessing the shoals from the cliff edged coast was dangerous and from the 1600s Carrick-a-Rede has been a stepping stone from which boats could work. Even today a rope bridge is put across the 60 foot chasm in time for 17 March and dismantled when the season ends on

13 September. With all fish stocks decreasing, so it is at Carrick-a-Rede. With the peak fishing period lasting three or four weeks, a good day would have brought in 300 fish, but this has fallen dramatically in recent years. The last good year was 1962, when the average rate was 400 per day. Traditionally the fish are held in ice at Ballycastle and shipped the following day to market in Manchester.

Orkney has its Old Man of Hoy and Antrim its basalt columned Chimney Tops; both are the result of tidal and wind erosion. Legend carries the tale of the weak intellect boy who on the death of his mother climbed the 40 foot high Chimney to be closer to her in Heaven. To the surprise of his neighbours he not only spent the whole night on the top, but descended safely the following morning.

Left: Taken from the pathway above Port Reostan, this photograph of the Giant's Harp with the Chimney Tops beyond illustrates the drama of the Causeway. It shows also, in the sweeping line of the Harp, how the lava flowed from fissures and not in an eruption. This part of the path is no longer accessible.

Left: Beached drontheims in the natural harbour at Portnaboe, 'the cow's inlet'. As the nineteenth century progressed, through the summer these boats would have carried more sightseers than fish. When the novelist William Makepeace Thackeray visited the Causeway in 1842, his boat trip cost him an exorbitant ten shillings. Learning that the word drontheim derives from Trondheim, the Norwegian town, begs the question – what were they doing on the Antrim coast? The design was copied from the double ended, clinker built Norwegian ships which from the late seventeenth century brought the ice which was used to keep fish fresh on its way to the English markets. The Norwegian design had itself come from the Viking longship.

Below Causeway Head, at the western end of the Causeway, lies Portcoon (or *Port Cung* – 'narrow port or inlet') Cave. Formed by tidal erosion along a fault line in the basalt, this was one of the great attractions for early visitors to the Causeway – and an additional source of income to the enterprising boatmen. This photograph shows a party entering the cave. Hugh McLaughlan, who lived at Carnside, close by the Causeway, is on the right with his gun and net. When boat parties were inside the cave they would have heard the booming echo of his gun, and on emerging would have been presented with his collecting net. Taken there in the morning, he was uplifted in the evening – unless the boatmen, after a good day, were tempted to a celebratory drink (something which was known to have happened from time to time).

Under the shadow of Aird Snout, at the west end of Port Noffer (*Port an Aifir* – 'the Giant's port'), this house was built by the Lecky family in 1863 on Townland of Aird, which came to them through marriage in the 1790s. Their connection with the Causeway caused many difficulties over the years. They demolished a memorial pillar raised by Lord Mark Kerr and they built this house despite objections from Lord Antrim – 'It is more on public, than on private grounds . . . Lord Antrim is desirous of preserving this magnificent specimen of the beauties of the country [in all its original grandeur]'. The Leckys also started the controversial Giant's Causeway Company. They owned the house until 1941 and twenty years later, when the National Trust bought the site, both it and the railings around it were swept away.

In July 1897 plans were announced by the Leckys to fence in the Causeway and make an admission charge. The holes for the iron pillars, cast in Belfast, were already being dug. Within a week, Mr F.N. Cooke, newly appointed secretary to the

Giant's Causeway Company Ltd (raised on £350 capital in fully paid up shares), announced that Mr Hugh Lecky (from whom they leased the land for £135 per annum) held the ground under an 'old fee farm, granted at the head court' and that as the Causeway could only be appreciated by those who could afford to go out in boats, he and a few personal friends had formed a company to carry out necessary improvements. Cooke insisted that in charging a nominal toll the company's purpose was not profit, but merely an attempt to recoup their outlay. Locals would have free admission and there would be free days at least once a week for the poorer classes. Some doubted the motives of this altruistic venture and later some 'trespassers', including Mr S.C. M'Ilroy, honorary secretary of the Ballymoney subcommittee of the Giant's Causeway Defence Committee, were issued with writs for not paying the admission fee. An action was started, but later abandoned, against these trespassers. The National Preservation Society then became involved and found that the Causeway Company consisted of 'seven persons, principally lawyers and related to one another' whose motive was profit (the Causeway attracted 80,000 visitors per annum). In April 1897, the society took their case before the Vice Chancellor's Court at Dublin but judgement went in favour of the company. All visitors would now pay sixpence. The railings – and the admission charge – were only removed when the National Trust took charge of the site.

Hugh Lecky's controversial house in the early 1890s, before the erection of the railings. Although the house was owned by the Lecky family, there is no evidence of them having actually lived there. In *Burke's Landed Gentry*, they appear as Lecky of Beardiville, a house which still stands on the Coleraine to Bushmills road, their progenitor being Hugh Lecky, High Sheriff of Antrim from 1835. His son, who leased the Causeway house to the company, was born in 1839 and was a justice of the peace. The last of the line, Jackie Lecky, died a bachelor some years ago.

In 1842, and long before his novel *Vanity Fair* made him a household name, William Makepeace Thackeray (1811–1863) was commissioned to write a travelogue on Ireland. Of his visit to the Causeway that autumn, he wrote caustically of the 'old grey hag' at the Wishing Well who had been there for hundreds and hundreds of years, selling her whiskey and never having change for a shilling. The old lady in this photograph from the 1890s may well have been a descendant. Thackeray's account, *The Irish Sketch-Book*, was first published the following year and ran to many editions.

Wishing Well, Giants Causeway

Taken in 1928, this photograph shows a party at the Wishing Well with Mrs Martin attending to the visitors. Her husband, a fisherman in the off season, was a guide on the Causeway. There was a small charge for the beaker of water, the promise that any wish would be fulfilled, and the tot of whiskey. The spring still runs from its catchment area high on Aird Snout, but is no longer safe to drink.

At the Wishing Chair Giant's Causeway

Three souvenir sellers at the Wishing Chair on the Little Causeway in the late 1890s. Unfortunately, nineteenth century accounts of the 'tourist industry' at the Causeway were written by visitors who had scant knowledge of the guides, the boatmen, the porters, and of these ladies, and never thought to record their names. This trio, either singly or as a group, were photographed frequently. In all photographs featuring her, the one on the right is never without her pipe!

That this young girl was photographed at the Wishing Chair with her dog is unique and possibly she was local – the Causeway photographers are not known to have used animals.

Taken between the Middle and the Grand Causeway, this trio are standing amongst the debris left from the days when the Causeway was quarried, while the boulders behind them are of crystalline basalt. In times past, lengths of the basaltic columns were used for buildings and gateposts in the immediate neighbourhood, and in the building of the ancient church of Templastragh at Port Braddan. The metal ores, particularly aluminium and iron, found in the red soil deposits between the lava flow, were exploited between the 1860s and the 1920s, and also for a short period during the Second World War.

This three generation group at the Giant's Loom were photographed by Lee of Portrush. Founded in the 1880s by Alexander Lee, the firm had premises in Main Street and Causeway View until the 1980s, and also a shop in nearby Coleraine. They also had a seasonal, but no doubt lucrative, business on the Causeway, operating from a hut at the Wishing Well.

This couple, again photographed at the Wishing Chair, confirms that not all photographers said 'Smile, please!' Each photographer had his 'pitch', rented from the Lecky family. While Alexander Lee operated from the Loom, the unknown photographer of this shot had the Wishing Chair.

Giants Loom, Giants Causeway.

M. 108.

On the east side of the Grand Causeway peninsula, under Aird Snout, the coastal path passes the Giant's Loom as it turns down into Port Noffer.

Portrush Rocket Life Saving Company, who were volunteers under coastguard management, used this Wreck Post on Ramore Head (*rath an mor* – 'great fort') for their quarterly practice exercises (one of which was always carried out in darkness). With the post representing a ship's mast, a Boxer Rocket (named after the military engineer, Captain Boxer) could carry a line up to 200 yards from 'shore' to the team at the 'mast'. A whip and whip block was pulled to the mast, then a hawser, i.e. a heavier rope, was secured to the whip and hauled to the post. This hawser was untied and secured to the mast above the whip block. When secure the Breeches Buoy was hauled out to the 'mast'. In a real situation the crew would then be pulled ashore, one by one. The exercise would typically last two hours, for which the members were paid. Founded in 1822 as a branch of the Revenue Service, the coastguard was transferred to the Admiralty around 1856 and soon their 300 teams around the coast, including the one at Portrush, were performing more rescues than the RNLI, and by the end of the nineteenth century had saved 14,000 lives with their rocket, line and Breeches Buoy. Although this post survived only until the early 1930s, the Breeches Buoy was used until 1988, when it was wholly superseded by the Sea King helicopter which is able to fly in bad weather.